MYSTERIES OF SPACE

INVESTIGATE!

WILL THE SUN BURN OUT?

BY ANNA COLLINS

Enslow PUBLISHING

Please visit our website, www.enslow.com.
For a free color catalog of all our high-quality books, call toll free 1-800-398-2504 or fax 1-877-980-4454.

Cataloging-in-Publication Data
Names: Collins, Anna.
Title: Will the sun burn out? / Anna Collins.
Description: New York : Enslow Publishing, 2024. | Series: Mysteries of space | Includes glossary and index.
Identifiers: ISBN 9781978535305 (pbk.) | ISBN 9781978535312 (library bound) | ISBN 9781978535329 (ebook)
Subjects: LCSH: Sun–Juvenile literature. | Sun–Evolution–Juvenile literature.
Classification: LCC QB539.E8 C65 2024 | DDC 523.7–dc23

Portions of this work were originally authored by Michael Sabatino and published as *How Long Will the Sun Last?* All new material this edition authored by Anna Collins.

Published in 2024 by
Enslow Publishing
2544 Clinton Street
Buffalo, NY 14224

Designer: Tanya Dellaccio Keeney
Editor: Jennifer Lombardo

Photo credits: Cover (logo) AAVAA/Shutterstock.com; series background Molibdenis/Shutterstock.com; cover janez volmajer/Shutterstock.com; p. 5 (top) Evgeny Atamanenko/Shutterstock.com; p. 5 (bottom) VectorMine/Shutterstock.com; pp. 7, 13, 15, 17, 19 courtesy of NASA; p. 9 Siberian Art/Shutterstock.com; p. 11 joshimerbin/Shutterstock.com; p. 21 djgis/Shutterstock.com; p. 22 muratart/Shutterstock.com; p. 23 Daniel Eskridge/Shutterstock.com; p. 25 Ali Jabber/Shutterstock.com; p. 27 Pike-28/Shutterstock.com; p. 29 Fortis Design/Shutterstock.com.

Printed in the United States of America

CPSIA compliance information: Batch #CSENS24: For further information contact Enslow Publishing at 1-800-398-2504.

CONTENTS

Words in the glossary appear in **bold** type the first time they are used in the text.

AN IMPORTANT STAR

Our sun is the closest star to our planet. It gives us light and heat—even on cloudy or cold days. Without the sun, life couldn't have started on Earth.

Earth's distance from the sun is very important. If it were closer, the planet would be very hot and all the water would boil away. If it were farther away, the planet would be very cold and all the water would freeze. Because we're at a distance that's just right, people sometimes call our position the "Goldilocks zone."

EXPLORE MORE!

ANOTHER NAME FOR THE GOLDILOCKS ZONE IS THE **HABITABLE** ZONE. OTHER STARS HAVE A HABITABLE ZONE, BUT SO FAR, SCIENTISTS HAVEN'T FOUND LIFE ON ANY OF THE PLANETS IN THOSE OTHER ZONES.

PEOPLE OFTEN FEEL HAPPIER AND LESS SLEEPY ON SUNNY DAYS. SUNLIGHT ALSO HELPS OUR BODY MAKE A SUBSTANCE CALLED VITAMIN D THAT'S IMPORTANT FOR STRONG BONES.

BIRTH AND DEATH

Stars aren't living, but they do have what we call a life cycle. Every star is "born" when a cloud of gas and dust called a nebula starts to collect into a ball. This ball burns for billions or trillions of years, then "dies" when it runs out of **fuel**.

Our sun was born about 4.5 billion years ago. One day it will burn out, like all stars. Luckily, that won't start happening until 5 billion years from now. No one who's alive today will be around when that happens!

EXPLORE MORE!

A BILLION SECONDS IS 32 YEARS, AND A BILLION HOURS IS ABOUT 115,000 YEARS. IT'S HARD TO IMAGINE HOW LONG EVEN 1 BILLION YEARS IS, LET ALONE 5 BILLION.

THIS PICTURE SHOWS THE CARINA NEBULA, WHERE NEW STARS ARE IN THE PROCESS OF BEING BORN.

CREATING THE SOLAR SYSTEM

Like other stars, our sun was born in a nebula. **Gravity** caused the nebula's material to clump together at some point in history. Over time, this matter formed a round, spinning mass called a protostar.

The protostar became **denser** and hotter, forming the core, or center, of the sun. Almost all the matter in the nebula was pulled into the core. The leftover matter formed planets, moons, and everything else in the **solar system**. The sun's gravity pulled these objects to it, causing them to circle, or orbit, the sun.

SOLAR SYSTEM PLANETS AND THEIR MOONS

LARGER PLANETS HAVE MORE GRAVITY, SO THEY TEND TO ATTRACT MORE MOONS.

EXPLORE MORE!

THE LAST FOUR PLANETS IN THE SOLAR SYSTEM ARE MADE OF GAS AND ICE INSTEAD OF ROCK LIKE THE FIRST FOUR. IF THEY WERE ANY CLOSER TO THE SUN, THE GAS AND ICE WOULDN'T HAVE BEEN ABLE TO STAND UP TO ITS HEAT.

A MEDIUM-SIZED STAR

The sun is huge compared to Earth and the other planets, but it's not very big for a star. Some stars are much smaller than our sun, and many are much, much larger.

One of the brightest stars we can see in the sky is called Betelgeuse. It's 1,400 times larger than the sun. If Betelgeuse were our sun, it would be big enough to swallow Jupiter and all the planets before it—and it's not even the biggest star we know of!

EXPLORE MORE!

BETELGEUSE IS FAR ENOUGH AWAY FROM EARTH THAT IT WON'T HURT EARTH WHEN IT DIES. HOWEVER, BECAUSE IT'S SO BIG, IT WILL CREATE A BEAUTIFUL LIGHT SHOW TO SEE IN THE SKY.

THIS PICTURE SHOWS THE SIZE DIFFERENCE BETWEEN THE SUN AND THE PLANETS IN OUR SOLAR SYSTEM.

BURNING UP

Stars die when they burn through all their fuel. A larger star has more fuel, but it burns through it faster than a smaller star does. This is because larger stars are generally hotter.

A star's color is a clue to how hot it is. Cooler stars are red, warmer stars—such as our sun—are orange or yellow, and the hottest stars are blue or white. Because our star is medium-sized, it's also medium-warm and will last for a medium amount of time.

EXPLORE MORE!

THE COOLEST STAR WE KNOW OF WAS NAMED CFBDSIR 1458 10B BY SCIENTISTS. IT'S A TYPE OF STAR CALLED A BROWN DWARF, AND IT'S 206°F (97°C)—A LITTLE WARMER THAN A FRESH CUP OF COFFEE.

THIS PICTURE, TAKEN IN 2020 BY NASA'S HUBBLE SPACE **TELESCOPE**, SHOWS STARS THAT ARE DIFFERENT COLORS AND AGES.

HOLDING STEADY

The sun is in the part of its life called the main sequence. Most of the other stars in our **galaxy**, which is called the Milky Way, are also main-sequence stars. During the main sequence, a star is in a state of balance. The inward pull of the star's gravity is matched by the outward flow of **energy** it creates as it burns fuel. This energy is the light and heat that we receive from the sun.

At some point, one of these forces will overpower the other. This will be the end of the sun's main-sequence stage.

EXPLORE MORE!

A STAR ENTERS THE MAIN SEQUENCE WHEN IT STARTS TURNING HYDROGEN INTO HELIUM IN ITS CORE. IT LEAVES THE MAIN SEQUENCE WHEN IT RUNS OUT OF HYDROGEN AND STARTS TURNING HELIUM INTO CARBON AND OXYGEN.

THE MILKY WAY IS A **SPIRAL** GALAXY LIKE THIS ONE. WE HAVE NO PICTURES OF THE WHOLE MILKY WAY BECAUSE WE'RE INSIDE IT. WE CAN ONLY TAKE PICTURES OF OTHER GALAXIES.

BECOMING A GIANT

The sun has enough fuel to stay in its main sequence for about another 5 billion years. However, when it runs out of hydrogen, that won't be the end of its life. At that point, the sun will turn into what scientists call a red giant. It'll grow larger and brighter.

The sun will get up to 1,000 times wider than it is today, and its core will get hotter as this happens. However, its surface will get cooler, making it look red. This is because the energy it puts out will be spread out over a larger area.

EXPLORE MORE!

IF OUR SUN WERE BIGGER, IT WOULD TURN INTO WHAT'S CALLED A RED SUPERGIANT AFTER IT LEAVES THE MAIN SEQUENCE. BETELGEUSE IS A RED SUPERGIANT.

SCIENTISTS BELIEVE EARTH MAY BECOME SOMETHING LIKE VENUS (SHOWN HERE) BEFORE THE SUN BECOMES A RED GIANT.

As the red-giant sun grows, it will swallow Mercury and Venus. It might also swallow Earth and even Mars. Scientists aren't sure if that will happen. However, even if Earth doesn't get swallowed, the sun will be too close. It will be too hot for anything to live on the planet anymore.

When the sun runs out of helium to burn, it will die. Its outer **layers** will blow away into space, possibly becoming a nebula. Its core will shrink to about the size of Earth and become what's called a white dwarf star.

EXPLORE MORE!

SCIENTISTS BELIEVE THE SUN WILL BE A RED GIANT FOR ABOUT 1 BILLION YEARS BEFORE IT BECOMES A WHITE DWARF. IT COULD STAY A WHITE DWARF FOR TRILLIONS OF YEARS UNTIL IT BURNS OUT COMPLETELY.

ONE DAY, THE SUN MAY CREATE A NEBULA SIMILAR TO THIS ONE, WHICH IS CALLED THE HELIX NEBULA.

SLOW AND STEADY

When people think of the sun becoming a red giant, they often picture it happening very suddenly. From a star's point of view, it does. However, from a human's point of view, it takes a very long time.

The time between the main sequence and the red giant **phase** is called the subgiant phase. Some scientists believe that it will take about 200 million years for the subgiant sun to get big enough to overtake any planets. That means the sun will grow more slowly than any living thing on Earth!

EXPLORE MORE!

LIKE STARS, PLANETS CHANGE MUCH MORE SLOWLY THAN LIVING THINGS AND LAST MUCH LONGER. FOR EXAMPLE, IT TAKES MILLIONS OF YEARS FOR MOUNTAINS TO FORM ON EARTH.

IT TAKES EIGHT MINUTES FOR THE SUN'S LIGHT TO REACH EARTH. EVEN IF SOMETHING HAPPENED TO THE SUN VERY QUICKLY, WE WOULDN'T KNOW ABOUT IT UNTIL EIGHT MINUTES LATER.

HOTTER AND HOTTER

Although we have several billion years before the sun becomes a red giant, scientists believe we have only about 1 billion years left on the planet. This is because the sun is getting 10 percent brighter every billion years.

As the sun gets brighter, it also gets hotter. A 10 percent increase in heat might not sound like a lot, but it's enough to make a difference. Life on Earth depends on a very **delicate** balance. Any change to the way things are now can change life for everything and everyone on the planet.

EXPLORE MORE!

WHEN THE EARTH GETS TOO COLD, IT CREATES WHAT WE CALL AN ICE AGE. SCIENTISTS BELIEVE THERE HAVE BEEN AT LEAST FIVE BIG ICE AGES IN THE PLANET'S HISTORY. IT ONLY TAKES A GLOBAL DROP OF ABOUT 10°F (5°C) TO CREATE AN ICE AGE.

ABOUT 100,000 YEARS AGO, THE EARTH STARTED TO GET COLDER. ANIMALS SUCH AS THESE WOOLLY MAMMOTHS ADAPTED, OR CHANGED, BY GROWING FUR. WHEN THE PLANET WARMED UP LATER, THEY COULDN'T ADAPT QUICKLY ENOUGH AND DIED OUT.

A 10 percent increase in the sun's light and heat will cause the habitable zone to move. Within 2 billion years, Mars will be in the habitable zone and Earth will be too hot.

A billion years is still a long time, and scientists are working on backup plans for humanity, such as looking for other planets humans could live on. Until they find one and figure out how to get there, people need to take care of Earth to make sure it doesn't get much warmer than it is now.

EXPLORE MORE!

SINCE 1880, HUMAN ACTIONS HAVE MADE EARTH ABOUT 1.7°F (1°C) WARMER ON AVERAGE. THIS IS CALLED CLIMATE CHANGE. THIS TINY CHANGE HAS CAUSED A LOT OF PROBLEMS, SUCH AS WORSE STORMS, MELTING ICE CAPS, AND LESS FOOD FOR PEOPLE AND ANIMALS.

RIGHT NOW, THE PLANET IS GETTING WARMER BECAUSE OF THINGS HUMANS ARE DOING, NOT BECAUSE THE SUN IS CHANGING. MANY PEOPLE ARE ASKING LAWMAKERS TO FIND WAYS TO PUT A STOP TO IT.

LIFE AS WE KNOW IT

When the solar system was created, Earth didn't look anything like it does now. It was so hot that nothing could live on it. Over a few hundred million years, it cooled down enough for oceans to form. A few hundred million years after that, life began.

Life on Earth won't be possible after the sun becomes a red giant. But, as the sun gets bigger, its habitable zone will move outward. It's possible that Pluto or another far-off icy rock could follow the same steps early Earth did.

EXPLORE MORE!

SOME SCIENTISTS BELIEVE THAT INSTEAD OF BECOMING EARTH-LIKE, PLUTO WILL BE FRIED BY THE ENERGY COMING OFF OF THE BIGGER SUN. WE DON'T KNOW FOR SURE WHAT WILL HAPPEN.

THIS PICTURE SHOWS WHAT EARTH MIGHT HAVE LOOKED LIKE WHEN IT WAS FIRST FORMED.

YEARS FROM NOW

In 2022, scientists found the first known planet in the habitable zone of a white dwarf star. This shows that after the sun dies, it might be possible for humans to live on a space object, such as Pluto, that's currently very far away from the sun. However, this is just a theory, or an idea that hasn't been proven yet.

Scientists have a very long time to get ready for the sun's increase in heat, and an even longer time to get ready for its death. By the time the planet isn't fit to live on, humans and animals will probably be living somewhere else!

LIFE ON ANOTHER PLANET WON'T BE EXACTLY LIKE LIFE ON EARTH. HOWEVER, HUMANS ARE GOOD AT ADAPTING TO CHANGES.

EXPLORE MORE!

PLANETS OUTSIDE OUR SOLAR SYSTEM ARE CALLED EXOPLANETS. SCIENTISTS HAVE FOUND A FEW THAT HUMANS MIGHT BE ABLE TO LIVE ON. THEY'RE WORKING ON WAYS TO GET TO THOSE PLANETS.

GLOSSARY

delicate: Easily harmed.

dense: Packed very closely together.

energy: Power used to do work.

fuel: Something used to make energy, heat, or power.

galaxy: A large group of stars, planets, gas, and dust that form a unit within the universe.

gravity: The force that pulls objects toward each other.

habitable: Able to support life.

layer: One thickness of something lying over or under another.

phase: A stage in a process or sequence of events.

solar system: The sun and all the space objects that orbit it, including the planets and their moons.

spiral: A shape or line that curls outward from a center point.

telescope: A tool that makes faraway objects look bigger and closer.

FOR MORE INFORMATION

BOOKS

Jankeliowitch, Anne. *Solar System.* Cambridge, MA: Barefoot Books, 2019.

McAnulty, Stacy. *Sun!: One in a Billion.* New York, NY: Henry Holt and Company, 2018.

Seluk, Nick. *The Sun Is Kind of a Big Deal.* New York, NY: Scholastic, 2018.

WEBSITES

BrainPOP: Sun
www.brainpop.com/science/space/sun
Watch a movie, play games, and take quizzes to test your knowledge of the sun.

Ducksters: The Sun
www.ducksters.com/science/sun.php
Learn more about the sun and check out some cool photos.

Neal.Fun: Size of Space
neal.fun/size-of-space/
This website shows how objects in space, such as our sun and Betelgeuse, compare in size.

INDEX